T0380838

Grandma Bunny's Stories about Little Boys

CAROL OSBORN

Copyright © 2018 by Carol Osborn. 546434

ISBN: Softcover   978-1-5035-1985-5

All rights reserved. No part of this book may
be reproduced or transmitted in any form or by
any means, electronic or mechanical, including
photocopying, recording, or by any information storage
and retrieval system, without permission in writing from
the copyright owner.

Print information available on the last page

Rev. date: 08/25/2018

To order additional copies of this book, contact:
Xlibris
1-888-795-4274
www.Xlibris.com
Orders@Xlibris.com

Grandma Bunny's Stories about Little Boys

CAROL OSBORN

This is a story about twin brothers, Dustin and Austin, who have taught me, by their hard work, and doing what they can, to only use the word *"disabled"* when referring to a car or a sewing machine, and to use *"differently abled"* when referring to people.

Dustin and Austin are twin boys, born prematurely, weighing just one pound six ounces each. They both had several medical problems and spent much of their young lives in the NICU (Neonatal Intensive Care Unit) in incubators. Some of the doctors didn't think that the boys would survive, but their parents wanted their boys to live and grow strong so very much that they prayed long and often for their baby boys. Grandmas and grandpas, aunts and uncles, pastors and friends and just about everyone who knew them prayed, and even some folks who didn't know them prayed for the twin baby boys. Do you know how people like to buy gifts for new babies? Well, one of the boy's grandpas bought lifetime hunting licenses for each of them. Maybe that was his way of showing his faith that their prayers would be answered. And they were. Each of the boys had several surgeries very early in their lives, but they had praying parents who refused to give up on those two precious babies. Both of them were later diagnosed as having cerebral palsy.

When I met Dustin and Austin, they were just beginning second grade. Dustin had learned two important things in physical therapy that summer: he could walk several feet to his mother without his walker, and how to get up from the floor without furniture to lift himself on. Two great accomplishments! Austin was able to walk without a walker by this time, but Dustin still needed a walker to navigate around the school. Both boys still had some difficulty with balance and were likely to fall if bumped into, but they were strong and energetic, and willing to work hard for what most of us take for granted, just to function.

I had known other children with cerebral palsy, all were severely affected by the condition. One appeared to be physically and mentally unaffected by the disease, but was easily unbalanced and had frequent falls, sometimes leading to injuries, like my friend Mark. Mark came to our school to talk to the kids about helping kids with physical challenges. He said that in high school some kids would knock him down and scatter his books, thinking that was funny. But he finished college and became a teacher, then a newspaper reporter. One child asked him how he got here today, and he said that he drove his car. The child said, "You can drive?"

Mark said, "Sure I can, who do you think parks in all of those handicapped spaces?"

The two little girls I knew who had cerebral palsy were wheelchair-bound and unable to speak. I never really knew how well they could function mentally, as they didn't communicate with anyone other than family members, except with their eyes and facial expressions.

Austin was able to function in the regular classroom with an assistant, and could communicate with his teachers and peers, and aides verbally.

Dustin, Dad, Austin

Dustin could say four words and knew several signed words, but communication was more difficult for him, because the part of his brain that regulates speech was involved. He too, functioned in a regular classroom with an assistant, but needed the assistance of technology, which his mother programmed for him to give his lunch requests, say and spell his spelling words, and communicate with classmates, including leading the class in the pledge to the American flag. I was fortunate to be his assistant.

Dustin caught a fish!

I always knew that Dustin was brighter than tests could measure, because although it took him longer to process what you asked him, and then to respond, his receptive skills were functioning well. Once, when his mother was talking on the telephone, she said, "Oh, I must have left it in the car." Dustin heard her and used his walker to get to a bench, moved the bench to the key rack and retrieved the key to his mother's car. He used his walker down the outside deck ramp, unlocked the car, and retrieved the item his mother was talking about. Then he locked the car and returned to the house up the ramp. He returned the car key to the key rack, the bench to its place, and handed his mother the item she'd left in the car while she was still on the telephone, much to her surprise!

Also, he had a sense of humor. He would laugh without a time delay if I showed him a silly picture, like a horse talking on the telephone, or an animal driving a car. That's another sign of intelligence.

I learned that stickers for good work didn't really impress Dustin, but that he was willing to work for a different motivator. A trip to the snack machine was both a break in the routine and a treat to eat! He would work harder to finish a task if I offered that! It was good exercise, he learned to choose and count the coins he would need from my hand, and his coordination improved inserting the coins and pushing the right buttons. I thought it was a win/win situation, until his next teacher decided that it wasn't fair for Dustin to have that opportunity that other children didn't have. I always thought that it wasn't fair for Dustin to have some of the disadvantages he had, and I was just trying to level the playing field for him whenever I could.

Both Austin and Dustin had visual difficulties and wore eyeglasses. Their physical education teacher did a great job of giving them alternatives they could achieve so they could be successful.

They left school early one afternoon a week for physical therapy, as well as having a different physical therapist twice a week at school. They also attended occupational therapy and speech therapy at school, including sign language. That's enough to wear out a kid with "normal abilities" whatever that is!

In the upper elementary grades, special education classes became available for Austin and Dustin. They both graduated from eighth grade and went to high school. In the summers, they worked in the garden and sold fresh produce. Tomatoes, squash, cucumbers, blueberries, what would you like? In 2013, Dustin and Austin graduated from high school.

Now Austin works in a hardware store, and in a veterinarian's office. Dustin works for Edward's Physical Therapy and volunteers at the hospital where his father works. Two nights a week they help take care of their grandfather, the one who bought them their lifetime hunting licenses.

So you see, they are still very busy and productive. Everyone who knows them is a better person for having known them. Students and classmates were always kinder to others after knowing Dustin and Austin.

I once had a friend who took offense at the term "disabled". She would say, "I'm not *disabled*, I'm *physically challenged*!" She wanted to know how she could help me when I was moving to a new apartment. I asked her if she could paint woodwork around kitchen windows. She said, "I can't reach up to do tops, and I can't bend down to do bottoms, but I'm really good at middles," with a smile.

That reminds me of Dustin and Austin. They can't do a few things, but they can do a lot of things, and what they can do, they do well! They give the best hugs. They're real good at "middles".

Dustin and Austin have seen and done so many things that many of us haven't. They've been to the racetrack and met NASCAR drivers. They've been to Disney World, and Dollywood. They've been hunting, fishing, and rafting.

When I asked Austin for advice he'd give to other students, he said, "Just keep trying, and be nice to your teachers."

They have taught me, by their hard work, and doing what they can, to only use the word *"disabled"* when referring to a car or a machine, and even that's temporary. When referring to people, I say *"differently abled"*. And aren't we all?

This is baby Connor. He's only three months old.

He's sweet, smart, handsome, and just as good as gold.

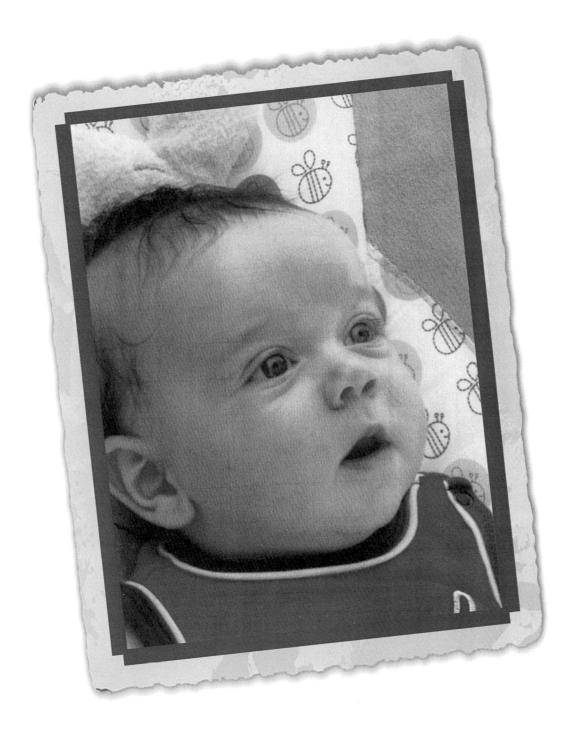

In the U.S. Marine Corps, his dad is a recruiter.

He's handsome in his uniform, but Connor is even cuter.

These little feet will have to grow so daddy's shoes he'll fill.

But Connor still has lots of time before he'll have to drill.

."Here I am with mom and dad. How do you like my sweater?"

"Just wait 'til you see my next suit, you'll like it even better!"

"I'm all dressed up to go to church to be baptized you know."

"It's silly to get all dressed up if you've no place to go."

"Mommy, will you teach me how to eat an ice cream cone?"

"Just stick your tongue way out like this. You won't have to eat it alone."

So I practiced and I practiced just like Mommy showed me how

Then I practiced more, and more,

and more and I CAN DO IT NOW!

Now it's my turn to pick and choose what we see on T.V.

Mickey Mouse or Muppets, I love the comedy!

It's been such a fun to watch you as you work and smile and play.

Now, close your eyes and rest awhile, you've had a busy day.

Dakota

When Dakota was a baby, he was surrounded by girls:

His mom, three sisters, and two grandmas. Guess which one got the curls?

Everyone wanted to hold him. He was such an adorable tot,

Until they found out whenever he drinks he sure throws up a lot!

Once, when he was a toddler they shut him in his room.

He got so mad he trashed it, his temper was his doom!

Toys everywhere, wallpaper torn, like an animal in a cage,

Bed unmade, things overturned. Oh, how Dakota did rage!

When he quieted down they went looking to find that sleepy-head.

Guess where they finally found him soundly sleeping under the bed.

Louie, You Can't Sing!

This is a very special story. Most stories have a beginning, a middle, and an ending. In the beginning, you learn about whom the story is written. In the middle you learn about the problem, or the goal of the story. Then the ending tells how the problem is solved, or how the goal is reached. But in this story, there are four possible endings!

Since every problem has more than one way that it can be solved, and different people might reach the same goal but in different ways, you may choose the ending that you like best, or write a new and even different ending of your own! This writer would like to know what you think – ocarolosborn@aol.com

When Louie turned five years old, it was time for him to go to school. He liked to count, and say his ABCs but most of all he loved to sing. He learned to say the pledge of allegiance to the American flag, loudly and clearly. He even knew how to stand up straight and tall when he said it. And he learned which hand was his right hand. His favorite color was black, because musical notes were black. His favorite shape was the triangle, because it was not only a shape, but also an instrument. It was a musical instrument in the shape of a triangle. Louie liked to dance, and boy, could he dance!

Louie had rhythm, and he could really beat those drums and tambourines, and rhythm sticks. He even liked to tap his pencil on his desk to help him think. But of course, he couldn't do that in school because that would distract the other children and disturb the teacher so that would be rude.

One day, the teacher said, "It is our class's turn to give a special program in the auditorium! We will be practicing our part of the program every day until you learn the songs and speaking parts."

Louie was so excited he couldn't wait to learn the songs and sing them with his classmates.

But, there was a problem. When Louie sang, he sang loud, and he sang clearly, but he didn't always sing the right notes!

Of course, he was just a little boy but the problem was that some of the other children would sing whatever Louie sang because his voice was loudest. Some of the children said, "Louie messed me up!"

One little girl said, "Louie, you're too loud."

And one little boy even said, "Louie, YOU CAN'T SING!"

Now, we all know that was rude and hurtful. Yes, they were just little kids but they didn't stop to think about how they would feel if someone said that to them. The teacher said that she heard some things while they were rehearsing that made her feel very disappointed.

"Children," she said, "I want you to listen to me very carefully and do not interrupt. You may ask questions when I'm finished, but not until then!

I believe that God has put every one of you and myself in this class for this year for a reason. It is so that we can help each other and learn from each other and to learn to be kind to others.

For five days of most weeks for this school year we are like a big family. We will learn that families work best when they cooperate and help each other. It is okay to compete with each other if it makes you try harder to be better at something, like running faster, or reading better, or playing games.

But if what you do or say is hurtful or untrue, or causes someone to feel bad about himself or herself, it is wrong. Every morning before you arrive, I sit at the desks of four or five of you and say a prayer for you to be successful today, to be and to feel safe, and to be helpful to yourself and others. By the end of every week I have prayed for each one of you individually. I believe in answered prayers.

"Before you speak, I want you to think, *'Is it kind? Is it true? Is it necessary?'*

If you cannot answer 'yes' to all three, don't say it!

If you cannot say 'yes' to *'Is it helpful?'* don't say it!

Now, if you can think of a way to help Louie to help this 'family', our class, to do better in our program, you may raise your hand and give your one suggestion, but only after you think about if it's kind, true, necessary, and helpful.

If not, I don't want to hear it.

Remember, I'm counting on you to make wise choices. You are never too young to practice making wise choices."

As the children gave their suggestions the teacher wrote them on the board. Even though the children couldn't all read yet, they were glad that they were allowed to think, and tried to be helpful.

Susie thought, "Maybe Louie should have a hearing test. She thought that since Louie sings so loudly, maybe he was hard of hearing like her Grandpa, who also speaks loudly.

Bobby thought, "Louie might need singing lessons. His big sister takes voice lessons and now she sings prettier.

Hope said "Since Louie does speak loudly and clearly, maybe he should have a speaking part instead of singing."

Paul said "Louie should dance instead of singing, because he was such a good dancer."

Mary said that the class should have a rhythm band play along with the singers. Some of the children could play, and some could sing.

ADD YOUR OWN SUGGESTIONS, THEN CHOOSE YOUR FAVORITE ENDING.

1. Louie had his ears checked by the school nurse. She said he had a wax buildup in both of his ears, and sent a note home to his parents, suggesting that they make an appointment with their doctor, and telling them when children's hearing would be checked at school. When Louie's doctor flushed the wax from his ears, he was able to hear better, and sing better.

2. Louie was given a speaking part in the program, and when the children sang, Louie learned how to be the conductor and wasn't required to sing. He learned to sing softly, but the microphones were all facing the other way.

3. When the teacher asked the children who would like to play in the rhythm band, six children volunteered. One played a drum, one played a tambourine, one played the bells, another played rhythm sticks, one played cymbals, and Louie played his favorite, the triangle. The children had lots of fun and learned cooperation.

4. Louie learned to practice listening. The library had c.d.s and d.v.d.s he could check out. Soon he could identify most of the instruments and their sounds. When he was seven and could read, he started taking piano lessons.

He learned to read music, and followed the notes. He continued to take music lessons through high school, and after college, he became a music teacher.

WHICH ENDING DO YOU LIKE BEST? WHY? MAKE UP ANOTHER ENDING OF YOU OWN.

Email it to the author at: Ocarolosborn@aol.com